# Bright Afghans

LEISURE ARTS, INC. • Maumelle, Arkansas

# Sugar Free

EASY

**Finished Size:** 47½" x 64"
(120.5 cm x 162.5 cm)

## SHOPPING LIST

### Yarn (Medium Weight) 4

[5.29 ounces, 270 yards
(150 grams, 247 meters) per skein]:

- ☐ Blue - 5 skeins
- ☐ Pink - 4 skeins
- ☐ Green - 4 skeins

### Crochet Hook

- ☐ Size I (5.5 mm)
  **or** size needed tor gauge

## GAUGE INFORMATION

In pattern,
(sc, ch 1) 7 times = 3¼" (8.25 cm)
and 12 rows = 4¼" (10.75 cm)

**Gauge Swatch:** 4½" (11.5 cm) square
With Pink, ch 20.
Work same as Afghan Body, page 5,
for 13 rows.

## STITCH GUIDE

**TREBLE CROCHET *(abbreviated tr)***

YO twice, insert hook in sc indicated, YO and pull up a loop (4 loops on hook), (YO and draw through 2 loops on hook) 3 times ***(Figs. 11a & b, page 47)***.

Each row is worked across length of Afghan Body. When joining yarn and finishing off, leave an 8" (20.5 cm) length to be worked into fringe.

## AFGHAN BODY

With Pink, ch 276.

**Row 1** (Wrong side)**:** Sc in second ch from hook, ★ ch 1, skip next ch, sc in next ch; repeat from ★ across; finish off: 138 sc and 137 ch-1 sps.

***Note:*** Loop a short piece of yarn around **back** of any stitch on Row 1 to mark **right** side.

**Row 2:** With **right** side facing and working in Front Loops Only ***(Fig. 2, page 44)***, join Blue with sc in first sc ***(see Joining With Sc, page 44)***; (ch 1, sc in next sc) across.

**Rows 3-5:** Ch 1, turn; working in Back Loops Only ***(Fig. 2, page 44)***, sc in first sc, (ch 1, sc in next sc) across.

Finish off.

**Row 6:** With **right** side facing and working in Back Loops Only, join Green with sc in first sc; (ch 1, sc in next sc) across.

**Row 7:** Ch 4 **(counts as first dc plus ch 1, now and throughout)**, turn; working in Back Loops Only, ★ skip next sc, tr in next sc, ch 1, working **behind** tr just made, tr in skipped sc, ch 1; repeat from ★ across to last sc, dc in last sc; finish off: 136 tr and 137 ch-1 sps.

**Row 8:** With **right** side facing and working in Front Loops Only, join Blue with sc in first dc; ch 1, (sc in next tr, ch 1) across to last dc, sc in last dc: 138 sc and 137 ch-1 sps.

**Rows 9-11:** Ch 1, turn; working in Back Loops Only, sc in first sc, (ch 1, sc in next sc) across.

Finish off.

**Row 12:** With **right** side facing and working in Back Loops Only, join Pink with sc in first sc; (ch 1, sc in next sc) across.

**Row 13:** Ch 4, turn; working in Back Loops Only, ★ skip next sc, tr in next sc, ch 1, working **behind** tr just made, tr in skipped sc, ch 1; repeat from ★ across to last sc, dc in last sc; finish off: 136 tr and 137 ch-1 sps.

**Row 14:** With **right** side facing and working in Front Loops Only, join Blue with sc in first dc; ch 1, (sc in next tr, ch 1) across to last dc, sc in last dc: 138 sc and 137 ch-1 sps.

**Rows 15-132:** Repeat Rows 3-14, 9 times; then repeat Rows 3-12 once **more**.

**Row 133:** Ch 1, turn; working in Back Loops Only, sc in first sc, (ch 1, sc in next sc) across; do **not** finish off.

# TRIM

## First Side

Ch 1, turn; slip st in both loops of first sc, (slip st, ch 2, dc) in next ch-1 sp, ★ skip next ch-1 sp, (slip st, ch 2, dc) in next ch-1 sp; repeat from ★ across to last 2 ch-1 sps, skip next ch-1 sp, slip st in last ch-1 sp and in both loops of last sc; finish off.

## Second Side

With **right** side facing and working in free loops of beginning ch ***(Fig. 3, page 44)***, join Pink with slip st in ch at base of first sc; (slip st, ch 2, dc) in next ch, ★ skip next 3 chs, (slip st, ch 2, dc) in next ch; repeat from ★ across to last 5 chs, skip next 3 chs, slip st in last 2 chs; finish off.

Holding 3 strands of corresponding color yarn together, each 16" (40.5 cm) long, add additional fringe across short edges of Afghan Body ***(Figs. 4a & b, page 45)***, using photo as a guide for placement.

# Beach Volley

EASY

**Finished Size:** 49" x 63½"
(124.5 cm x 161.5 cm)

## SHOPPING LIST

### Yarn (Medium Weight) MEDIUM 4

[5 ounces, 236 yards
(141 grams, 215 meters) per skein]:

☐ Variegated - 6 skeins

[7 ounces, 364 yards
(198 grams, 333 meters) per skein]:

☐ Blue - 4 skeins
☐ Green - 3 skeins

### Crochet Hook

☐ Size H (5 mm)
**or** size needed for gauge

## GAUGE INFORMATION

In pattern,
(dc, ch 1) 5 times = 3¼" (8.25 cm)
and 12 rows = 5¼" (13.25 cm)

**Gauge Swatch:** 5½" (14 cm) square

With Variegated, ch 20.

Work same as Afghan Body, page 11, for 12 rows.

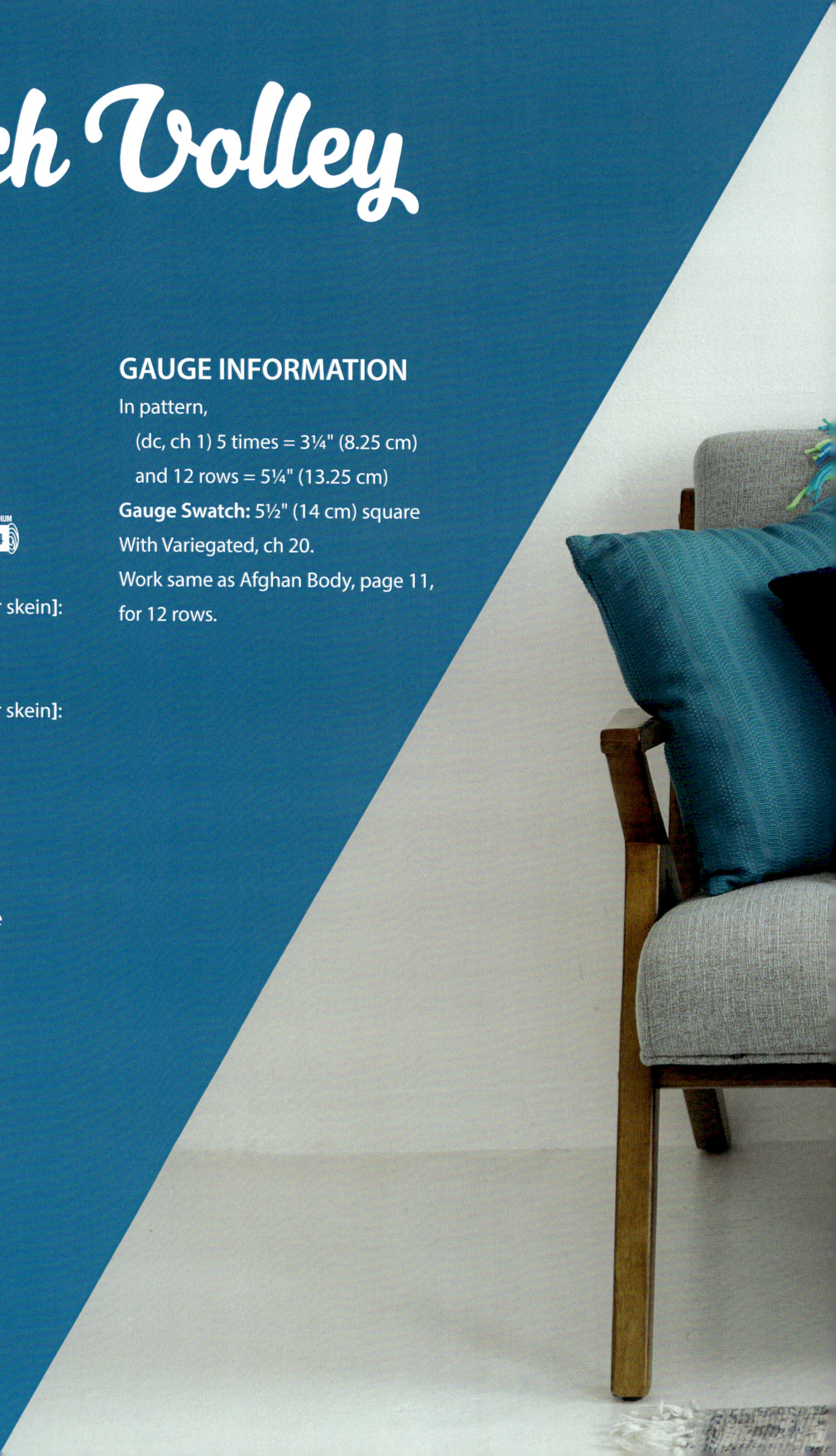

## STITCH GUIDE

**DOUBLE TREBLE CROCHET**

***(abbreviated dtr)***

YO 3 times, insert hook in ch indicated, YO and pull up a loop (5 loops on hook), (YO and draw through 2 loops on hook) 4 times ***(Figs. 12a & b, page 47)***.

Each row is worked across length of Afghan Body. When joining yarn and finishing off, leave an 8" (20.5 cm) length to be worked into fringe.

## AFGHAN BODY

With Variegated, ch 198; place marker in fourth ch from hook for st placement.

**Row 1** (Right side)**:** Dc in sixth ch from hook, ★ ch 1, skip next ch, dc in next ch; repeat from ★ across; finish off: 97 dc and 97 sps.

***Note:*** Loop a short piece of yarn around any stitch to mark Row 1 as **right** side.

**Row 2:** With **wrong** side facing, join Blue with sc in first dc ***(see Joining With Sc, page 44)***; ★ dtr in top 2 loops of next ch ***(Fig. A)***, sc in next dc; repeat from ★ across, dtr in top 2 loops of next ch, sc in next ch; finish off: 98 sc and 97 dtr.

**Fig. A**

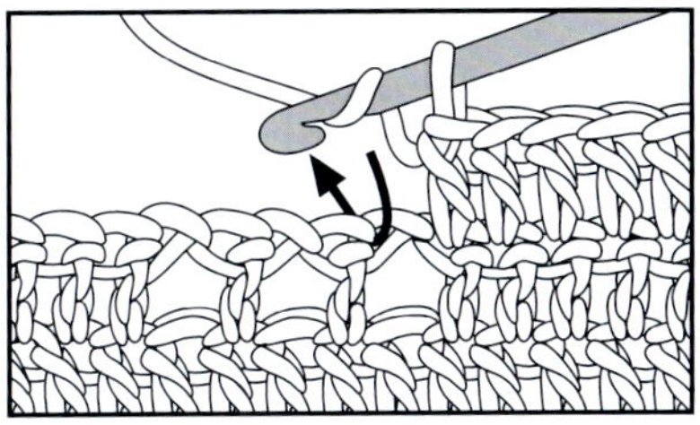

**Row 3:** With **right** side facing, join Variegated with dc in first sc ***(see Joining With Dc, page 44)***; ★ ch 1, skip next dtr, dc in next sc; repeat from ★ across; finish off: 98 dc and 97 ch-1 sps.

**Row 4:** With **wrong** side facing, join Green with sc in first dc; (dtr in top 2 loops of next ch, sc in next dc) across; finish off: 98 sc and 97 dtr.

**Row 5:** With **right** side facing, join Variegated with dc in first sc; ★ ch 1, skip next dtr, dc in next sc; repeat from ★ across; finish off: 98 dc and 97 ch-1 sps.

**Row 6:** With **wrong** side facing, join Blue with sc in first dc; (dtr in top 2 loops of next ch, sc in next dc) across; finish off: 98 sc and 97 dtr.

**Row 7:** With **right** side facing, join Variegated with dc in first sc; ★ ch 1, skip next dtr, dc in next sc; repeat from ★ across; finish off: 98 dc and 97 ch-1 sps.

Repeat Rows 4-7 for pattern until Afghan Body measures approximately 48½" (123 cm) from beginning ch, ending by working Row 7.

# TRIM

## First Side

With **right** side facing, join Variegated with slip st in first dc on last row worked; (slip st in next ch-1 sp, ch 1) across to last ch-1 sp, slip st in last ch-1 sp and in last dc; finish off.

## Second Side

With **right** side facing and working in sps and in free loops of beginning ch ***(Fig. 3, page 44)***, join Variegated with slip st in first ch; (slip st in next sp, ch 1) across to last sp, slip st in last sp and in marked ch; finish off.

Holding 2 strands of corresponding color yarn together, each 16" (40.5 cm) long, add additional fringe in each row across short edges of Afghan Body ***(Figs. 4a & b, page 45)***.

# Oops My Nails

EASY

**Finished Size:** 49" x 67"
(124.5 cm x 170 cm)

## SHOPPING LIST

### Yarn (Medium Weight) MEDIUM 4

[5 ounces, 256 yards
(141 grams, 234 meters) per skein]:

- ☐ Purple - 6 skeins
- ☐ Dk Pink - 5 skeins

### Crochet Hook

- ☐ Size I (5.5 mm)
  **or** size needed for gauge

## GAUGE INFORMATION

In pattern,
7 repeats = 6¾" (17.25 cm)
and 8 rows = 4" (10 cm)
**Gauge Swatch:** 4¼" (10.75 cm) square
With Purple, ch 15.
Work same as Afghan Body, page 17, for 9 rows.

## STITCH GUIDE

**CLUSTER** (uses next 4 chs)

Pull up a loop in each of next 4 chs, YO and draw through all 5 loops on hook.

Each row is worked across length of Afghan Body. When joining yarn and finishing off, leave a 7" (18 cm) length to be worked into fringe.

## AFGHAN BODY

With Purple, ch 210.

**Row 1** (Right side)**:** Sc in second ch from hook and in next ch, ★ ch 4, skip next 2 chs, sc in next ch; repeat from ★ across; finish off: 71 sc and 69 ch-4 sps.

***Note:*** Loop a short piece of yarn around any stitch to mark Row 1 as **right** side.

**Row 2:** With **wrong** side facing and working in Back Loops Only ***(Fig. 2, page 44)***, join Purple with sc in first sc ***(see Joining With Sc, page 44)***; work Cluster, ch 4, ★ skip next sc, work Cluster, ch 4; repeat from ★ across to last 2 sc, skip next sc, hdc in last sc; finish off: 69 Clusters and 69 ch-4 sps.

**Row 3:** With **right** side facing and working in Front Loops Only ***(Fig. 2, page 44)***, join Purple with sc in first hdc; work Cluster, ch 4, ★ skip next Cluster, work Cluster, ch 4; repeat from ★ across to last 2 sts, skip next Cluster, hdc in last sc; finish off.

**Row 4:** With **wrong** side facing and working in Back Loops Only, join Dk Pink with sc in first hdc; work Cluster, ch 4, ★ skip next Cluster, work Cluster, ch 4; repeat from ★ across to last 2 sts, skip next Cluster, hdc in last sc; finish off.

**Row 5:** With **right** side facing and working in Front Loops Only, join Dk Pink with sc in first hdc; work Cluster, ch 4, ★ skip next Cluster, work Cluster, ch 4; repeat from ★ across to last 2 sts, skip next Cluster, hdc in last sc; finish off.

**Row 6:** With **wrong** side facing and working in Back Loops Only, join Purple with sc in first hdc; work Cluster, ch 4, ★ skip next Cluster, work Cluster, ch 4; repeat from ★ across to last 2 sts, skip next Cluster, hdc in last sc; finish off.

**Row 7:** With **right** side facing and working in Front Loops Only, join Purple with sc in first hdc; work Cluster, ch 4, ★ skip next Cluster, work Cluster, ch 4; repeat from ★ across to last 2 sts, skip next Cluster, hdc in last sc; finish off.

**Rows 8-94:** Repeat Rows 4-7, 21 times; then repeat Rows 4-6 once **more**.

**Row 95:** With **right** side facing and working in Front Loops Only, join Purple with sc in first hdc; work Cluster, ch 2, ★ skip next Cluster, work Cluster, ch 2; repeat from ★ across to last 2 sts, skip next Cluster, hdc in last sc; finish off: 69 Clusters and 69 ch-2 sps.

**Row 96:** With **wrong** side facing and working in both loops, join Purple with sc in first hdc; ch 2, ★ skip next 2 chs, sc in next Cluster, ch 2; repeat from ★ across to last 4 sts, skip next 2 chs, sc in last Cluster and in last sc; do **not** finish off: 209 sts.

## TRIM

### First Side

Ch 1, turn; (slip st, ch 2, dc) in first sc, ★ skip next sc and next ch, (slip st, ch 2, dc) in next ch; repeat from ★ across to last 4 sts, skip next sc and next ch, slip st in last 2 sts; finish off.

### Second Side

With **right** side facing and working in chs and in free loops of beginning ch ***(Fig. 3, page 44)***, join Purple with slip st in first ch; (slip st, ch 2, dc) in next ch, ★ skip next 2 chs, (slip st, ch 2, dc) in next ch; repeat from ★ across; finish off.

Holding 4 strands of corresponding color yarn together, each 14" (35.5 cm) long, add additional fringe in end of each color stripe across short edges of Afghan Body ***(Figs. 4a & b, page 45)***.

# Super Diva

EASY

**Finished Size:** 49" x 64"
(124.5 cm x 162.5 cm)

## SHOPPING LIST

### Yarn (Medium Weight) MEDIUM 4

[3.5 ounces, 220 yards
(100 grams, 200 meters) per skein]:

☐ Purple - 5 skeins
☐ Dk Pink - 5 skeins
☐ Pink - 5 skeins
☐ Black - 3 skeins

### Crochet Hook

☐ Size H (5 mm)
**or** size needed for gauge

### Additional Supplies

☐ Yarn needle

## GAUGE INFORMATION

In pattern,
5 repeats (20 sts) = 5¼" (13.25 cm)
One Strip = 3¼" wide x 64" high
(8.25 cm x 162.5 cm)
**Gauge Swatch:** 3¼" wide x 5" high
(8.25 cm x 12.75 cm)
With Purple, ch 20.
Work same as Strip A, page 23.

## STITCH GUIDE

**TREBLE CROCHET** ***(abbreviated tr)***
YO twice, insert hook in st indicated, YO and pull up a loop (4 loops on hook), (YO and draw through 2 loops on hook) 3 times ***(Figs. 11a & b, page 47)***.

**BOBBLE**
Ch 4, sc in second ch from hook, 2 dc in next ch, sc in last ch, fold first sc on top of last sc and slip st in skipped ch. Keep Bobble to **right** side.

Each row is worked across length of Strip. When joining yarn and finishing off, leave an 8" (20.5 cm) length to be worked into fringe.

## STRIP A (Make 5)

### First Half

With Purple, ch 244.

**Row 1** (Right side)**:** Sc in second ch from hook, ch 1, skip next ch, sc in next ch, ★ work Bobble, skip next ch, sc in next ch, ch 1, skip next ch, sc in next ch; repeat from ★ across: 122 sc, 60 Bobbles, and 61 ch-1 sps.

***Note:*** Loop a short piece of yarn around last Bobble made on Row 1 to mark **right** side and bottom edge.

**Row 2:** Ch 1, turn; sc in first sc, (ch 1, sc in next sec) across: 122 sc and 121 ch-1 sps.

**Row 3:** Ch 4 **(counts as first dc plus ch 1)**, turn; ★ skip next sc, tr in next sc, ch 1, working **behind** tr just made, tr in skipped sc, ch 1; repeat from ★ across to last sc, dc in last sc: 120 tr and 121 ch-1 sps.

**Row 4:** Ch 1, turn; sc in first dc, ch 1, (sc in next tr, ch 1) across to last dc, sc in last dc; finish off: 122 sc and 121 ch-1 sps.

**Row 5:** With **right** side facing, join Black with sc in first sc ***(see Joining With Sc, page 44)***; (ch 1, sc in next sc) across; finish off.

### Second Half

**Row 1:** With **right** side facing and working in free loops of beginning ch ***(Fig. 3, page 44)***, join Purple with dc in first ch ***(see Joining With Dc, page 44)***; ch 1, ★ skip next 3 chs, tr in next ch, ch 1, working in **front** of tr just made, tr in second skipped ch, ch 1; repeat from ★ 59 times **more**, skip next ch, dc in last ch: 120 tr and 121 ch-1 sps.

**Row 2:** Ch 1, turn; sc in first dc, ch 1, (sc in next tr, ch 1) across to last dc, sc in last dc; finish off: 122 sc and 121 ch-1 sps.

**Row 3:** With **right** side facing, join Black with sc in first sc; (ch 1, sc in next sc) across; finish off.

## STRIP B (Make 5)

Work same as Strip A replacing Purple with Dk Pink.

## STRIP C (Make 5)

Work same as Strip A replacing Purple with Pink.

## ASSEMBLY

Whipstitch Strips together as follows, placing Strips in the following order: (A, B, C) 5 times.

Place two Strips with **wrong** sides together and bottom edges at the same end. With Black, sew through both pieces once to secure the beginning of the seam, leaving an ample yarn end to weave in later. Working through **both** loops of each stitch on **both** pieces, insert the needle from **front** to **back** through first stitch and pull yarn through ***(Fig. A)***, ★ insert the needle from **front** to **back** through next stitch on both pieces and pull yam through; repeat from ★ across long edge.

Join remaining Strips in same manner.

## TRIM

### First Side

With **right** side of long edge facing, join Black with slip st in first sc; (slip st in next ch-1 sp, ch 1) across to last ch-1 sp, slip st in last ch-1 sp and in last sc; finish off.

### Second Side

Work same as First Side across second long edge.

Holding 3 strands of corresponding color yarn together, each 16" (40.5 cm) long, add additional fringe in each row across short edges of Afghan ***(Figs. 4a & b, page 45)***.

**Fig. A**

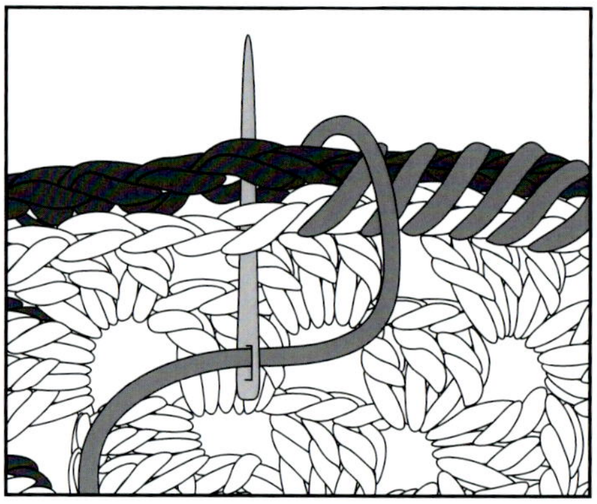

# Psychedelic

EASY

**Finished Size:** 48" x 64"
(122 cm x 162.5 cm)

## SHOPPING LIST

### Yarn (Medium Weight) 4

[7 ounces, 364 yards
(198 grams, 333 meters) per skein]:

- ☐ Blue - 3 skeins
- ☐ Yellow - 3 skeins
- ☐ Green - 3 skeins
- ☐ Pink - 3 skeins

### Crochet Hook

☐ Size I (5.5 mm)
**or** size needed for gauge

## GAUGE INFORMATION

In pattern,
(sc, ch 1) 4 times = 2½" (6.25 cm)
and 8 rows = 3" (7.5 cm)

**Gauge Swatch:** 4" (10 cm) square
With Blue, ch 14.
Work same as Afghan Body, page 29,
for 12 rows.

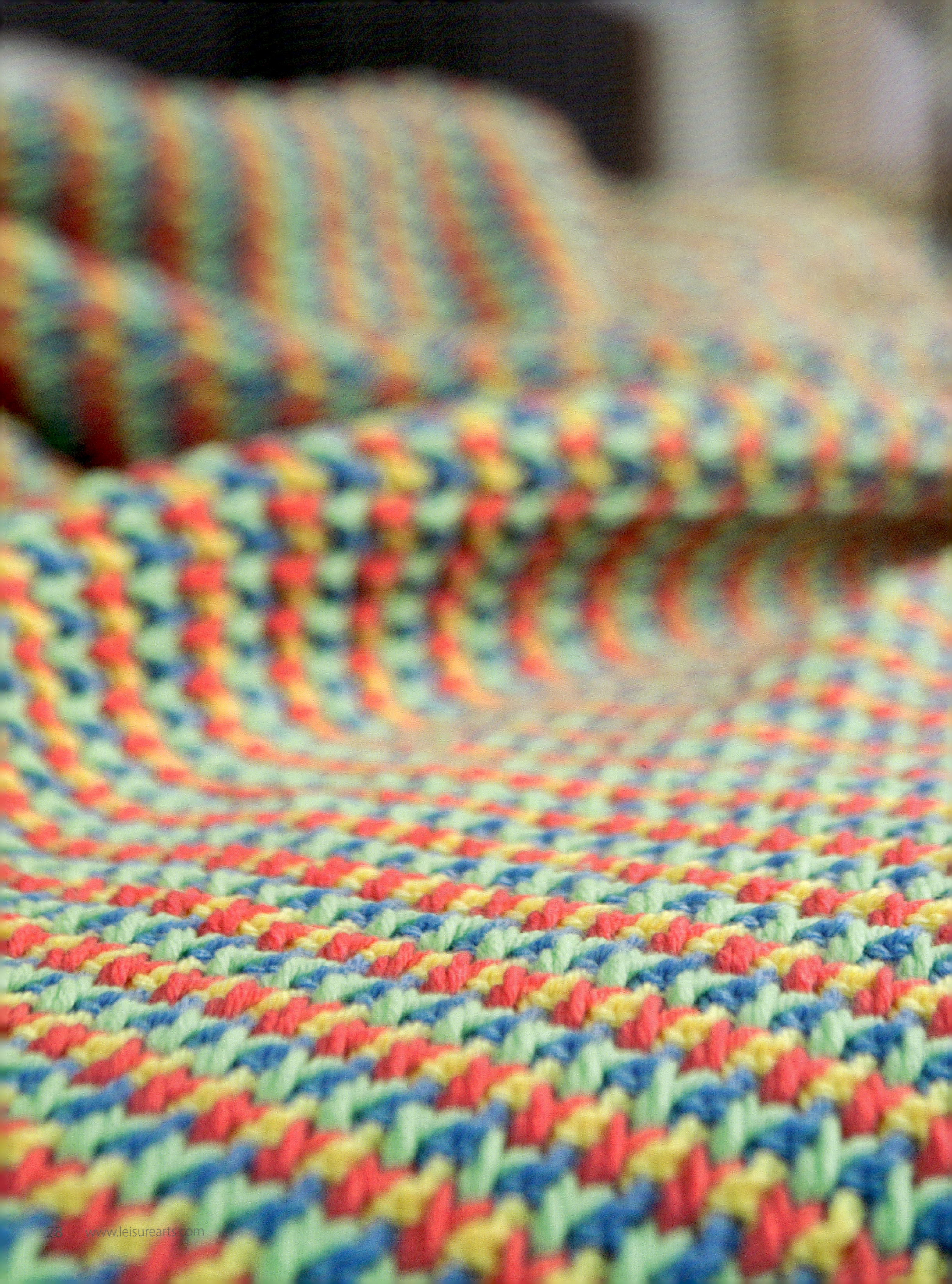

## STITCH GUIDE

**LONG DOUBLE CROCHET**
***(abbreviated LDC)***

YO, insert hook in st indicated ***(Fig. A)***, YO and pull up a loop even with last st made (3 loops on hook), (YO and draw through 2 loops on hook) twice.

**Fig. A**

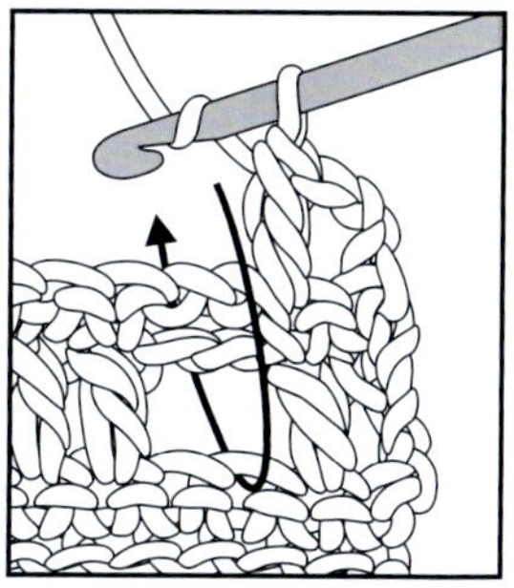

**FRONT POST DOUBLE CROCHET**
***(abbreviated FPdc)***

YO, insert hook from **front** to **back** around post of st indicated ***(Fig. B)***, YO and pull up a loop (3 loops on hook), (YO and draw through 2 loops on hook) twice. Skip st behind FPdc.

**Fig. B**

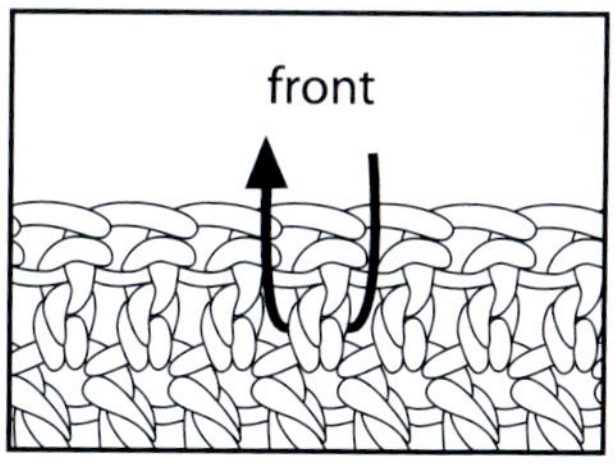


Each row is worked across length of Afghan Body. When joining yarn and finishing off, leave a 7" (18 cm) length to be worked into fringe.

## AFGHAN BODY

With Blue, ch 206.

**Row 1** (Right side)**:** Sc in second ch from hook, ★ ch 1, skip next ch, sc in next ch; repeat from ★ across; finish off: 103 sc and 102 chs.

***Note:*** Loop a short piece of yarn around any stitch to mark Row 1 as **right** side.

**Row 2:** With **wrong** side facing, join Blue with sc in first sc ***(see Joining With Sc, page 44)***; ★ ch 1, skip next ch, sc in next sc; repeat from ★ across; finish off.

**Row 3:** With **right** side facing, join Blue with sc in first sc; working in **front** of next ch ***(Fig. 1, page 44)***, work LDC in skipped ch one row **below**, ★ ch 1, skip next sc, working in **front** of next ch, work LDC in skipped ch one row **below**; repeat from ★ across to last sc, sc in last sc; finish off: 102 LDC and 101 chs.

**Row 4:** With **wrong** side facing, join Blue with sc in first sc; ★ sc in next LDC, working **behind** next ch ***(Fig. 1, page 44)***, work LDC in skipped sc one row **below**; repeat from ★ across to last 2 sts, sc in last 2 sts; finish off: 104 sc and 101 LDC.

**Row 5:** With **right** side facing, join Green with sc in first sc; working in **front** of next sc, work FPdc around st one row **below**, ★ ch 1, skip next LDC, working in **front** of next sc, work FPdc around st one row **below**; repeat from ★ across to last sc, sc in last sc; finish off: 102 FPdc and 101 chs.

**Row 6:** With **wrong** side facing, join Yellow with sc in first sc; ★ sc in next FPdc, working **behind** next ch, work LDC in skipped LDC one row **below**; repeat from ★ across to last 2 sts, sc in last 2 sts; finish off: 104 sc and 101 LDC.

**Row 7:** With **right** side facing, join Pink with sc in first sc; working in **front** of next sc, work FPdc around FPdc one row **below**, ★ ch 1, skip next LDC, working in **front** of next sc, work FPdc around FPdc one row **below**; repeat from ★ across to last sc, sc in last sc; finish off: 102 FPdc and 101 chs.

**Row 8:** With **wrong** side facing, join Blue with sc in first sc; ★ sc in next FPdc, working **behind** next ch, work LDC in skipped LDC one row **below**; repeat from ★ across to last 2 sts, sc in last 2 sts; finish off: 104 sc and 101 LDC.

Repeat Rows 5-8 for pattern until Afghan Body measures approximately 47" (119.5 cm) from beginning ch, ending by working Row 8.

**Last Row:** With right side facing, join Blue with sc in first sc; ★ ch 1, skip next sc, sc in next st; repeat from ★ across; finish off: 102 ch-1 sps.

## TRIM

### First Side

With **right** side facing, join Blue with slip st in first sc on Last Row; (slip st in next ch-1 sp, ch 1) across to last ch-1 sp, slip st in last ch-1 sp and in last sc; finish off.

### Second Side

With **right** side facing and working in sps and in free loops of beginning ch ***(Fig. 3, page 44)***, join Blue with slip st in first ch; (slip st in next sp, ch 1) across to last sp, slip st in last sp and in next ch; finish off.

For additional fringe, add one 14" (35.5 cm) strand of corresponding color yarn in each row across short edges of Afghan Body ***(Figs. 4a & b, page 45)***.

# So Fresh

EASY

**Finished Size:** 46½" 64"
(118 cm x 162.5 cm)

## SHOPPING LIST

### Yarn (Medium Weight) 4

[3.5 ounces, 180 yards
(100 grams, 165 meters) per skein]:

- ☐ Orange - 13 skeins
- ☐ Green - 4 skeins
- ☐ Yellow - 4 skeins

### Crochet Hook

- ☐ Size I (5.5 mm)

or size needed for gauge

## GAUGE INFORMATION

In pattern,
(sc, ch 1) 5 times = 3" (7.5 cm)
and 12 rows = 3⅞" (9.75 cm)

**Gauge Swatch:** 4" (10 cm) square
With Orange, ch 14.
Work same as Afghan Body, page 35, for 12 rows.

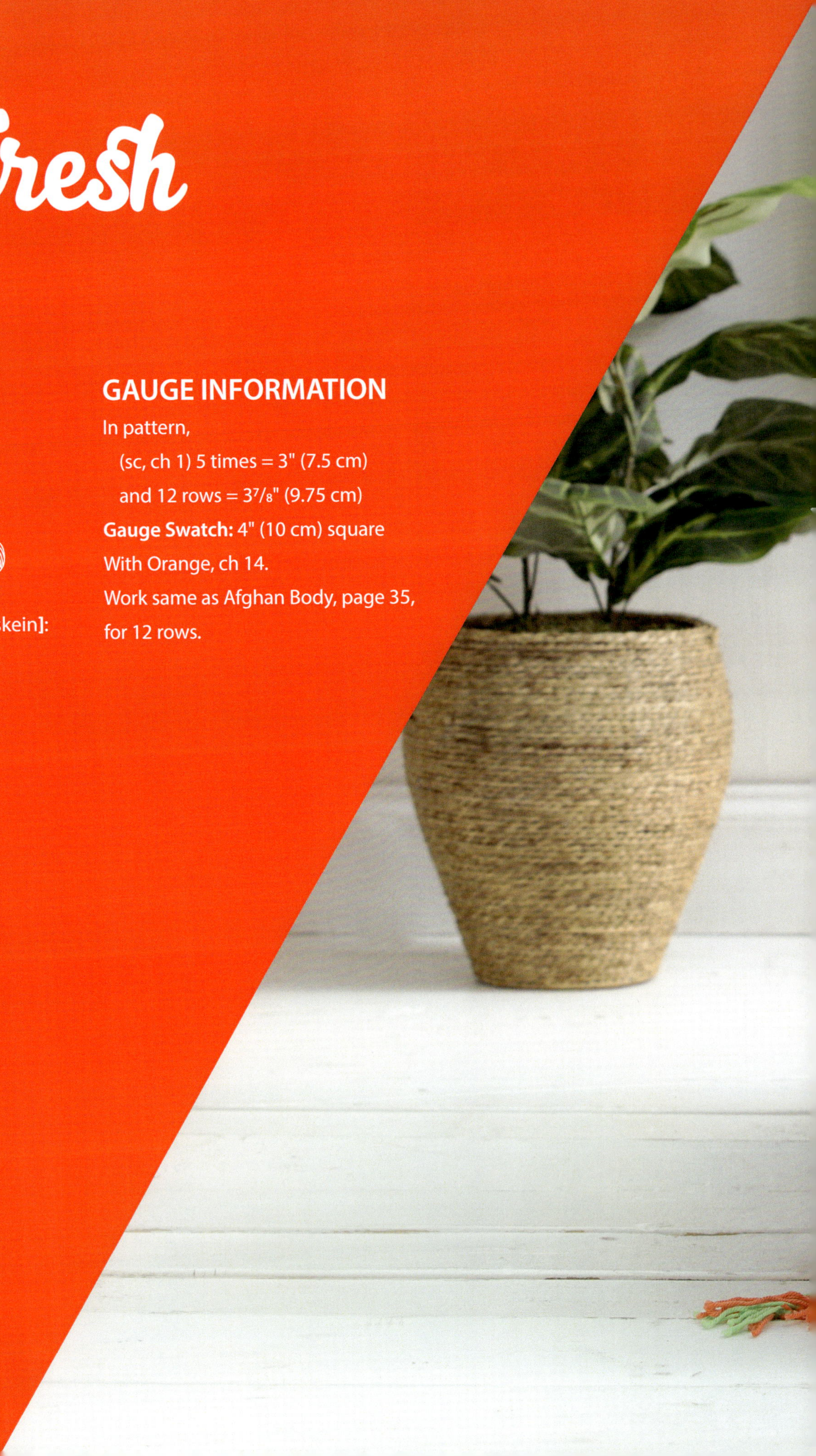

## STITCH GUIDE

**TREBLE CROCHET** ***(abbreviated tr)***

YO twice, insert hook in st indicated, YO and pull up a loop (4 loops on hook), (YO and draw through 2 loops on hook) 3 times ***(Figs. 11a & b, page 47)***.

Each row is worked across length of Afghan Body. When joining yarn and finishing off, leave a 7" (18 cm) length to be worked into fringe.

## AFGHAN BODY

With Orange, ch 214.

**Row 1** (Wrong side)**:** Sc in second ch from hook, ★ ch 1, skip next ch, sc in next ch; repeat from ★ across; finish off: 107 sc and 106 chs.

***Note:*** Loop as short piece of yarn around **back** of any stitch on Row 1 to mark **right** side.

**Row 2:** With **right** side facing, join Orange with sc in first sc ***(see Joining With Sc, page 44)***; sc in next ch and in each sc and each ch across; finish off: 213 sc.

**Row 3:** With **right** side facing, join Green with sc in first sc; ★ ch 1, skip next sc, sc in next sc; repeat from ★ across; finish off: 107 sc and 106 chs.

**Row 4:** With **right** side facing, join Green with sc in first sc; ★ skip next ch and next sc, working in **front** of next ch ***(Fig. 2, page 44)***, tr in sc one row **below**, sc in skipped sc; repeat from ★ across to last 2 sts, sc in last ch and in last sc; finish off: 108 sc and 105 tr.

**Row 5:** With **right** side facing, join Orange with sc in first sc; ch 1, ★ skip next tr, sc in next sc, ch 1; repeat from ★ across to last 2 sc, skip next sc, sc in last sc; finish off: 107 sc and 106 chs.

**Row 6:** With right side facing, join Orange with sc in first sc; ★ skip next ch and next sc, working in **front** of next ch, tr in st one row **below**, sc in skipped sc; repeat from ★ across to last 2 sts, sc in last ch and in last sc; finish off: 108 sc and 105 tr.

**Row 7:** With **right** side facing, join Yellow with sc in first sc; ch 1, ★ skip next tr, sc in next sc, ch 1; repeat from ★ across to last 2 sc, skip next sc, sc in last sc; finish off: 107 sc and 106 chs.

**Row 8:** With **right** side facing, join Yellow with sc in first sc; ★ skip next ch and next sc, working in **front** of next ch, tr in st one row **below**, sc in skipped sc; repeat from ★ across to last 2 sts, sc in last ch and in last sc; finish off: 108 sc and 105 tr.

**Row 9:** With **right** side facing, join Orange with sc in first sc; ch 1, ★ skip next tr, sc in next sc, ch 1; repeat from ★ across to last 2 sc, skip next sc, sc in last sc; finish off: 107 sc and 106 chs.

**Row 10:** With **right** side facing, join Orange with sc in first sc; ★ skip next ch and next sc, working in **front** of next ch, tr in st one row **below**, sc in skipped sc; repeat from ★ across to last 2 sts, sc in last ch and in last sc; finish off: 108 sc and 105 tr.

**Row 11:** With **right** side facing, join Green with sc in first sc; ch 1, ★ skip next tr, sc in next sc, ch 1; repeat from ★ across to last 2 sc, skip next sc, sc in last sc; finish off: 107 sc and 106 chs.

**Row 12:** With **right** side facing, join Green with sc in first sc; ★ skip next ch and next sc, working in **front** of next ch, tr in st one row **below**, sc in skipped sc; repeat from ★ across to last 2 sts, sc in last ch and in last sc; finish off: 108 sc and 105 tr.

**Row 13:** With **right** side facing, join Orange with sc in first sc; ch 1, ★ skip next tr, sc in next sc, ch 1; repeat from ★ across to last 2 sc, skip next sc, sc in last sc; finish off: 107 sc and 106 chs.

**Row 14:** With **right** side facing, join Orange with sc in first sc; ★ skip next ch and next sc, working in **front** of next ch, tr in st one row **below**, sc in skipped sc; repeat from ★ across to last 2 sts, sc in last ch and in last sc; finish off: 108 sc and 105 tr.

**Rows 15-18:** Repeat Rows 13 and 14 twice.

**Rows 19-28:** Repeat Rows 7-14 once, then repeat Rows 7 and 8 once **more**.

**Rows 29-34:** Repeat Rows 13 and 14, 3 times.

**Row 35:** With **right** side facing, join Green with sc in first sc; ch 1, ★ skip next tr, sc in next sc, ch 1; repeat from ★ across to last 2 sc, skip next sc, sc in last sc; finish off: 107 sc and 106 chs.

**Row 36:** With **right** side facing, join Green with sc in first sc; ★ skip next ch and next sc, working in **front** of next ch, tr in st one row **below**, sc in skipped sc; repeat from ★ across to last 2 sts, sc in last ch and in last sc; finish off: 108 sc and 105 tr.

**Rows 37-140:** Repeat Rows 5-36, 3 times; then repeat Rows 5-12 once **more**.

**Row 141:** With **right** side facing, join Orange with sc in first sc; sc in next tr and in each sc and each tr across; finish off: 213 sc.

**Row 142:** With **wrong** side facing, join Orange with sc in first sc; ★ ch 1, skip next sc, sc in next sc; repeat from ★ across; finish off: 107 sc and 106 ch-1 sps.

## TRIM

### First Side

With **right** side facing, join Orange with slip st in first sc on Row 142; (slip st in next ch-1 sp, ch 1) across to last ch-1 sp, slip st in last ch-1 sp and in last sc; finish off.

### Second Side

With **right** side facing and working in sps and in free loops of beginning ch *(Fig. 3, page 44)*, join Orange with slip st in ch at base of first sc; (slip st in next sp, ch 1) across to last sp, slip st in last sp and in last ch; finish off.

Holding 2 strands of corresponding color yarn together, each 14" (35.5 cm) long, add additional fringe in each color stripe across short edges of Afghan Body *(Figs. 4a & b, page 45)*.

# Meeting the Parallels

EASY

**Finished Size:** 49½" x 68" (125.5 cm x 172.5 cm)

## SHOPPING LIST

### Yarn (Medium Weight) MEDIUM 4

- ☐ Black - 39 ounces, 2,145 yards (1,110 grams, 1,961.5 meters)
- ☐ Blue - 12 ounces, 660 yards (340 grams, 603.5 meters)
- ☐ Pink - 12 ounces, 660 yards (340 grams,603.5 meters)
- ☐ Green - 12 ounces, 660 yards (340 grams, 603.5 meters)
- ☐ Yellow - 12 ounces, 660 yards (340 grams, 603.5 meters)

### Crochet Hooks

- ☐ Size H (5 mm) **and**
- ☐ Size I (5.5 mm)

**or** sizes needed for gauge

## GAUGE INFORMATION

With larger size hook, in pattern, (sc, ch 1) 5 times = 3" (7.5 cm) and 12 rows = 3¾" (9.5 cm)

**Gauge Swatch:** 6" wide x 4" high (15.25 cm x 10 cm)

With Black and using larger size hook, ch 21.

Work same as Afghan Body, page 41, for 12 rows.

Randell Cartwheeling in Thunderstorms
URBAN WATERCOLOR SKETCHING

## STITCH GUIDE

**TREBLE CROCHET *(abbreviated tr)***
YO twice, insert hook in ch indicated, YO and pull up a loop (4 loops on hook), (YO and draw through 2 loops on hook) 3 times ***(Figs. 11a & b, page 47)***.

Each row is worked across length of Afghan Body. When joining yarn and finishing off, leave an 8" (20.5 cm) length to be worked into fringe.

## AFGHAN BODY

With Black and using larger size hook, ch 227.

**Row 1** (Right side)**:** Sc in second ch from hook and in next ch,★ ch 1, skip next ch, sc in next ch; repeat from ★ across; finish off: 114 sc and 112 chs.

***Note:*** Loop a short piece of yarn around any stitch to mark Row 1 as **right** side.

**Row 2:** With **wrong** side facing and using larger size hook, join Black with sc in first sc ***(see Joining With Sc, page 44)***; ch 1, (sc in next sc, ch 1) across to last 2 sc, sc in last 2 sc; finish off.

**Row 3:** With **right** side facing and using larger size hook, join Blue with sc in first sc; ★ skip next sc, tr in top 2 loops of next ch ***(Fig. A)***, working **behind** tr just made, sc in skipped sc; repeat from ★ across to last sc, sc in last sc; finish off: 114 sc and 112 tr.

**Fig. A**

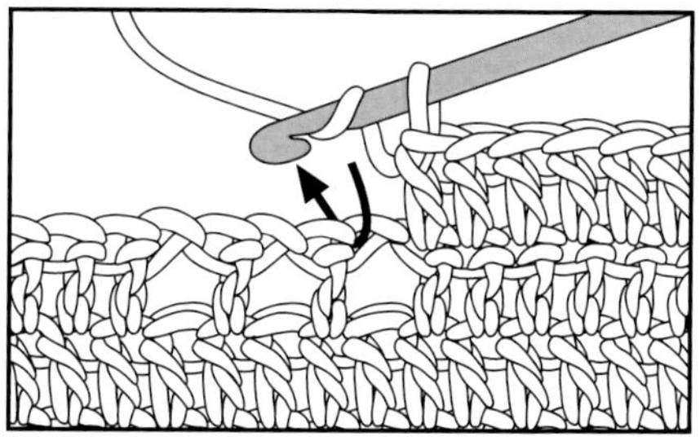

**Row 4:** With **right** side facing and using larger size hook, join Black with sc in first sc; ★ skip next tr, sc in next sc, ch 1; repeat from ★ across to last sc, sc in last sc; finish off: 114 sc and 112 chs.

**Row 5:** With **wrong** side facing and using larger size hook, join Black with sc in first sc; ch 1, (sc in next sc, ch 1) across to last 2 sc, sc in last 2 sc; finish off.

**Row 6:** With **right** side facing and using larger size hook, join Pink with sc in first sc; ★ skip next sc, tr in top 2 loops of next ch, working **behind** tr just made, sc in skipped sc; repeat from ★ across to last sc, sc in last sc; finish off: 114 sc and 112 tr.

**Row 7:** With **right** side facing and using larger size hook, join Black with sc in first sc; ★ skip next tr, sc in next sc, ch 1; repeat from ★ across to last sc, sc in last sc; finish off: 114 sc and 112 chs.

**Row 8:** With **wrong** side facing and using larger size hook, join Black with sc in first sc; ch 1, (sc in next sc, ch 1) across to last 2 sc, sc in last 2 sc; finish off.

**Row 9:** With **right** side facing and using larger size hook, join Green with sc in first sc; ★ skip next sc, tr in top 2 loops of next ch, working **behind** tr just made, sc in skipped sc; repeat from ★ across to last sc, sc in last sc; finish off: 114 sc and 112 tr.

**Row 10:** With **right** side facing and using larger size hook, join Black with sc in first sc; ★ skip next tr, sc in next sc, ch 1; repeat from ★ across to last sc, sc in last sc; finish off: 114 sc and 112 chs.

**Row 11:** With **wrong** side facing and using larger size hook, join Black with sc in first sc; ch 1, (sc in next sc, ch 1) across to last 2 sc, sc in last 2 sc; finish off.

**Row 12:** With **right** side facing and using larger size hook, join Yellow with sc in first sc; ★ skip next sc, tr in top 2 loops of next ch, working **behind** tr just made, sc in skipped sc; repeat from ★ across to last sc, sc in last sc; finish off: 114 sc and 112 tr.

**Row 13:** With **right** side facing and using larger size hook, join Black with sc in first sc; ★ skip next tr, sc in next sc, ch 1; repeat from ★ across to last sc, sc in last sc; finish off: 114 sc and 112 chs.

**Row 14:** With **wrong** side facing and using larger size hook, join Black with sc in first sc; ch 1, (sc in next sc, ch 1) across to last 2 sc, sc in last 2 sc; finish off.

**Rows 15-158:** Repeat Rows 3-14, 12 times.

## TRIM

### First Side

With **right** side facing and using smaller size hook, join Black with slip st in first sc on Row 158; ch 2, (slip st in next ch-1 sp, ch 2) across to last ch-1 sp, slip st in last ch-1 sp and in last sc; finish off.

### Second Side

With **right** side facing, using smaller size hook, and working in sps and in free loops of beginning ch ***(Fig. 3, page 44)***, join Black with slip st in first ch; (slip st in next sp, ch 2) across to chs at base of last 2 sc, slip st in next 2 chs; finish off.

Holding 3 strands of corresponding color yarn together, each 16" (40.5 cm) long, add additional fringe in each row across short edges of Afghan Body ***(Figs. 4a & b, page 45)***.

# General Instructions

## ABBREVIATIONS

| | |
|---|---|
| ch(s) | chain(s) |
| cm | centimeters |
| dc | double crochet(s) |
| dtr | double treble crochet(s) |
| FPdc | Front Post double crochet(s) |
| hdc | half double crochet(s) |
| LDC | Long Double Crochet(s) |
| mm | millimeters |
| sc | single crochet(s) |
| sp(s) | space(s) |
| st(s) | stitch(es) |
| tr | treble crochet(s) |
| YO | yarn over |

★ — work instructions following ★ as many **more** times as indicated in addition to the first time.

( ) or [ ] — work enclosed instructions **as many** times as specified by the number immediately following **or** work all enclosed instructions in the stitch or space indicated **or** contains explanatory remarks.

colon (:) — the number(s) given after a colon at the end of a row or round denote(s) the number of stitches or spaces you should have on that row or round.

| CROCHET TERMINOLOGY | | |
|---|---|---|
| UNITED STATES | | INTERNATIONAL |
| slip stitch (slip st) | = | single crochet (sc) |
| single crochet (sc) | = | double crochet (dc) |
| half double crochet (hdc) | = | half treble crochet (htr) |
| double crochet (dc) | = | treble crochet (tr) |
| treble crochet (tr) | = | double treble crochet (dtr) |
| double treble crochet (dtr) | = | triple treble crochet (ttr) |
| triple treble crochet (tr tr) | = | quadruple treble crochet (qtr) |
| skip | = | miss |

## GAUGE

Exact gauge is **essential** for proper size. Before beginning your Afghan, make the sample swatch given in the individual instructions in the yarn and hook specified. After completing the swatch, measure it, counting your stitches and rows carefully. If your swatch is larger or smaller than specified, **make another, changing hook size to get the correct gauge**. Keep trying until you find the size hook that will give you the specified gauge.

## JOINING WITH SC

When instructed to join with a sc, begin with a slip knot on the hook. Insert the hook in the stitch or space indicated, YO and pull up a loop, YO and draw through both loops on hook.

## JOINING WITH DC

When instructed to join with a dc, begin with a slip knot on the hook. YO, holding loop on hook, insert the hook in the stitch or space indicated, YO and pull up a loop (3 loops on hook), (YO and draw through 2 loops on hook) twice.

## WORKING IN FRONT OF, AROUND, OR BEHIND A STITCH

Work in stitch or space indicated, inserting hook in direction of arrow ***(Fig. 1)***.

## BACK OR FRONT LOOP ONLY

Work only in loop(s) indicated by arrow ***(Fig. 2)***.

## FREE LOOPS OF A CHAIN

When instructed to work in free loops of a chain, work in loop indicated by arrow ***(Fig. 3)***.

**Fig. 1**

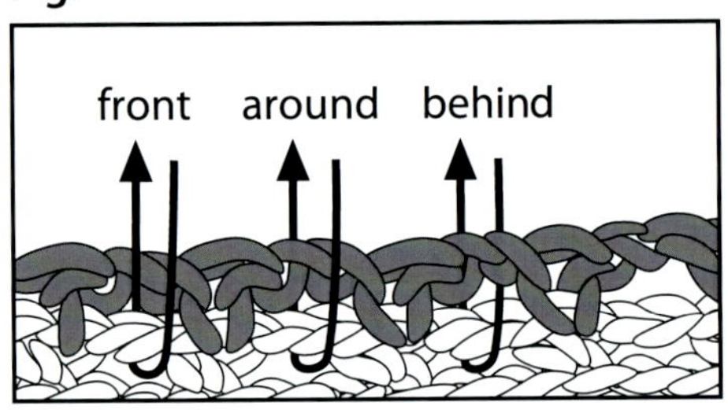


**Fig. 2**

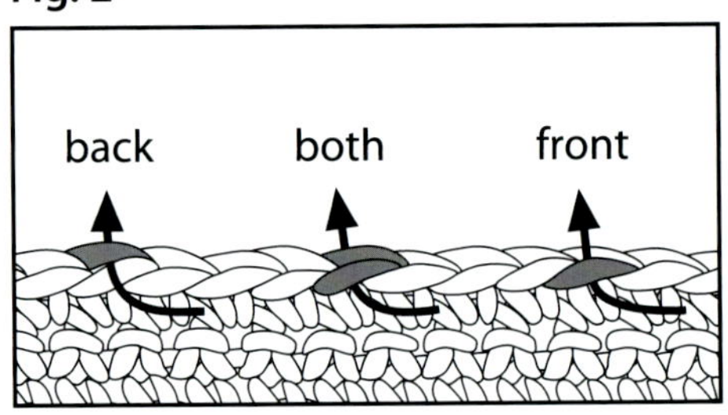


**Fig. 3**

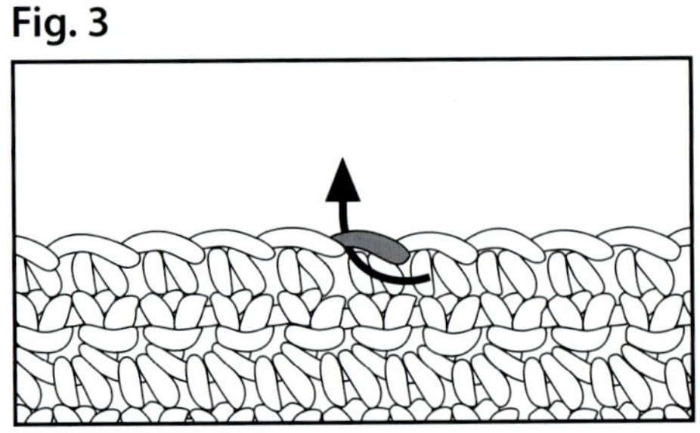

## FRINGE

Cut a piece of cardboard 6" (15 cm) wide and ½" (12 mm) longer than you want your finished fringe to be. Wind the yarn **loosely** and **evenly** lengthwise around the cardboard until the card is filled, then cut across one end; repeat as needed.

Hold together as many strands as specified in individual instructions; fold in half.

With **wrong** side facing and using a crochet hook, draw the folded end up through a row and pull the loose ends through the folded end ***(Fig. 4a)***; draw the knot up tightly ***(Fig. 4b)***. Repeat, spacing as specified in individual inst ructions.

Lay flat on a hard surface and trim the ends.

**Fig. 4a**

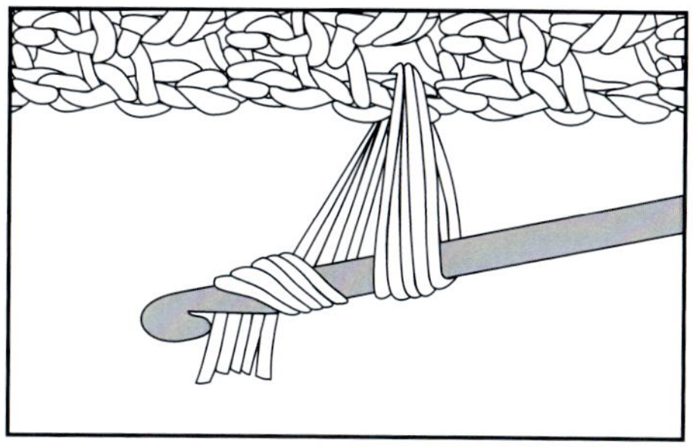

**Fig. 4b**

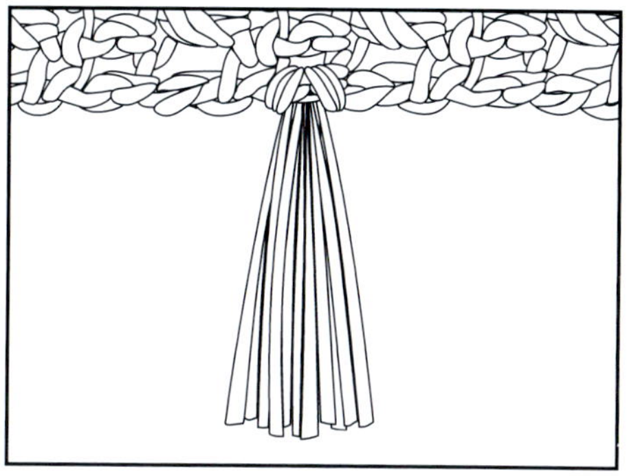

| Yarn Weight Symbol & Names | LACE 0 | SUPER FINE 1 | FINE 2 | LIGHT 3 | MEDIUM 4 | BULKY 5 | SUPER BULKY 6 | JUMBO 7 |
|---|---|---|---|---|---|---|---|---|
| Type of Yarns in Category | Fingering, size 10 crochet thread | Sock, Fingering, Baby | Sport, Baby | DK, Light Worsted | Worsted, Afghan, Aran | Chunky, Craft, Rug | Super Bulky, Roving | Jumbo, Roving |
| Crochet Gauge* Ranges in Single Crochet to 4" (10 cm) | 32-42 sts** | 21-32 sts | 16-20 sts | 12-17 sts | 11-14 sts | 8-11 sts | 6-9 sts | 5 sts and fewer |
| Advised Hook Size Range | Steel*** 6 to 8, Regular hook B-1 | B-1 to E-4 | E-4 to 7 | 7 to I-9 | I-9 to K-10½ | K-10½ to M/N-13 | M/N-13 to Q | Q and larger |

*GUIDELINES ONLY: The chart above reflects the most commonly used gauges and hook sizes for specific yarn categories.

** Lace weight yarns are usually crocheted with larger hooks to create lacy openwork patterns. Accordingly, a gauge range is difficult to determine. Always follow the gauge stated in your pattern.

*** Steel crochet hooks are sized differently from regular hooks–the higher the number, the smaller the hook, which is the reverse of regular hook sizing.

| | |
|---|---|
| ■□□□ **BASIC** | Projects using basic stitches. May include basic increases and decreases. |
| ■■□□ **EASY** | Projects may include simple stitch patterns, color work, and/or shaping. |
| ■■■□ **INTERMEDIATE** | Projects may include involved stitch patterns, color work, and/or shaping. |
| ■■■■ **COMPLEX** | Projects may include complex stitch patterns, color work, and/or shaping using a variety of techniques and stitches simultaneously. |

| **CROCHET HOOKS** | | | | | | | | | | | | | | | | | |
|---|---|---|---|---|---|---|---|---|---|---|---|---|---|---|---|---|---|
| **U.S.** | B-1 | C-2 | D-3 | E-4 | F-5 | G-6 | 7 | H-8 | I-9 | J-10 | K-10½ | L-11 | M/N-13 | N/P-15 | P/Q | Q | S |
| **Metric - mm** | 2.25 | 2.75 | 3.25 | 3.5 | 3.75 | 4 | 4.5 | 5 | 5.5 | 6 | 6.5 | 8 | 9 | 10 | 15 | 16 | 19 |

# Basic Stitches

## CHAIN

To work a chain stitch, begin with a slip knot on the hook. Bring the yarn over hook from **back** to **front**, catching the yarn with the hook and turning the hook slightly toward you to keep the yarn from slipping off. Draw the yarn through the slip knot ***(Fig. 5)*** **(first chain st made, *abbreviated ch*)**.

**Fig. 5**

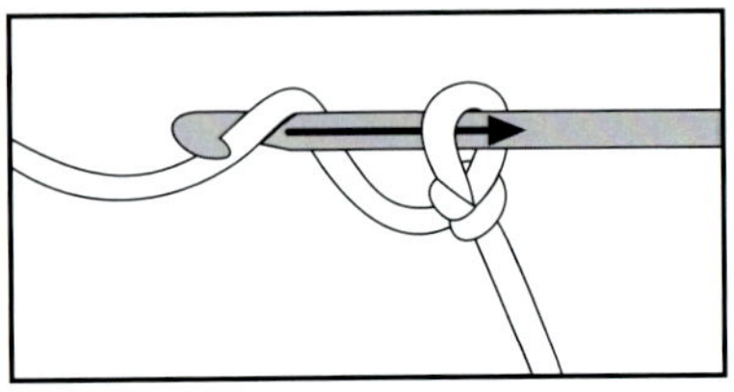

## WORKING INTO THE CHAIN

When counting chains, always begin with the first ch from the hook and then count toward the beginning of your foundation chain ***(Fig. 6a)***.

**Method 1:** Insert hook under top two strands of each chain ***(Fig. 6b)***.

**Method 2:** Insert hook into back ridge of each chain ***(Fig. 6c)***.

**Method 3:** To form a beginning ring, work the specified number of chains and then join to the first chain made with a slip st ***(Fig. 6d)***.

**Fig. 6a**

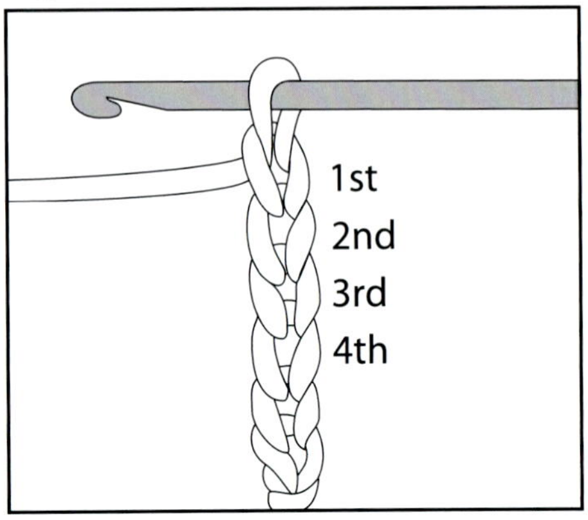


**Fig. 6b**

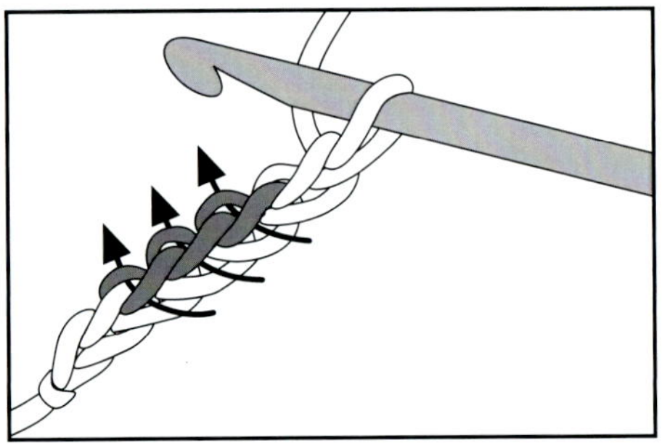

**Fig. 6c**

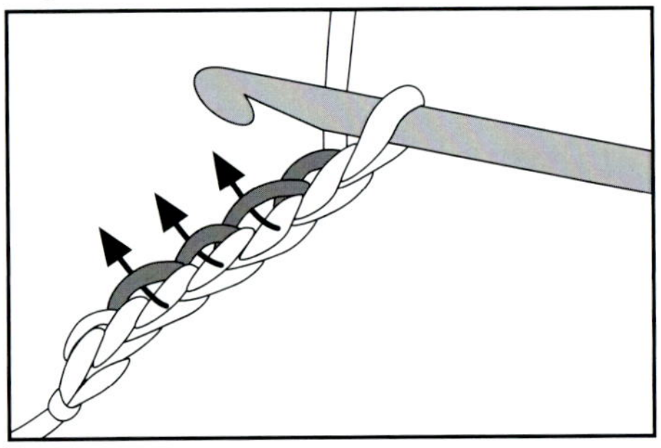

**Fig. 6d**

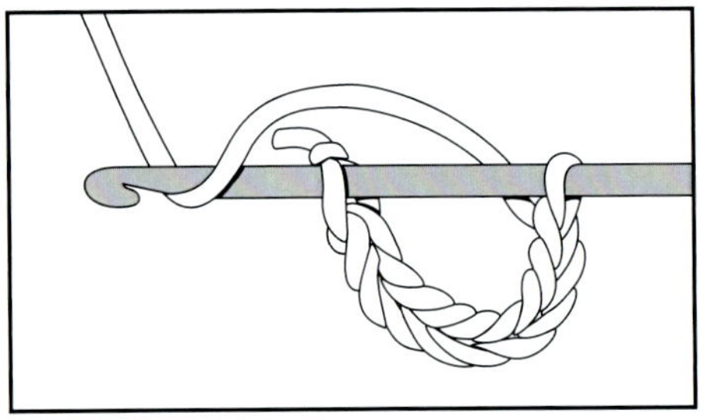

## SLIP STITCH

To work a slip stitch, insert hook in stitch or space indicated, YO and draw through stitch and through loop on hook ***(Fig. 7)*** **(slip stitch made, *abbreviated slip st*)**.

**Fig. 7**

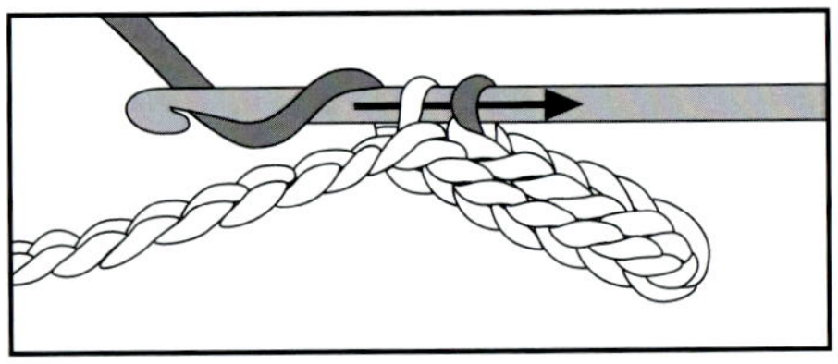

## SINGLE CROCHET

Insert hook in stitch or space indicated, YO and pull up a loop, YO and draw through both loops on hook ***(Fig. 8)*** **(single crochet made, *abbreviated sc*)**.

**Fig. 8**

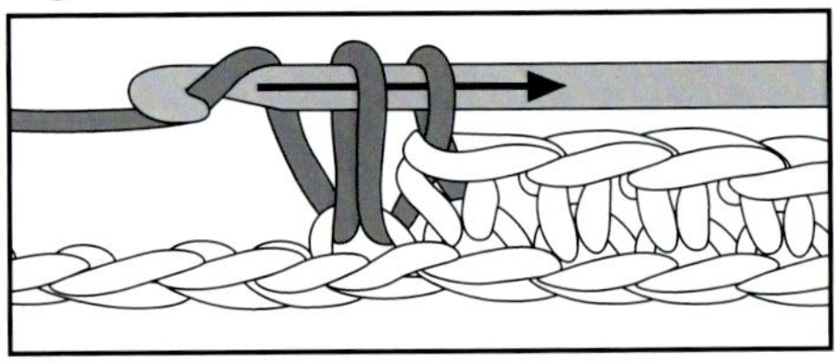

## HALF DOUBLE CROCHET

YO, insert hook in stitch or space indicated, YO and pull up a loop, YO and draw through all 3 loops on hook ***(Fig. 9)*** **(half double crochet made, *abbreviated hdc*)**.

**Fig. 9**

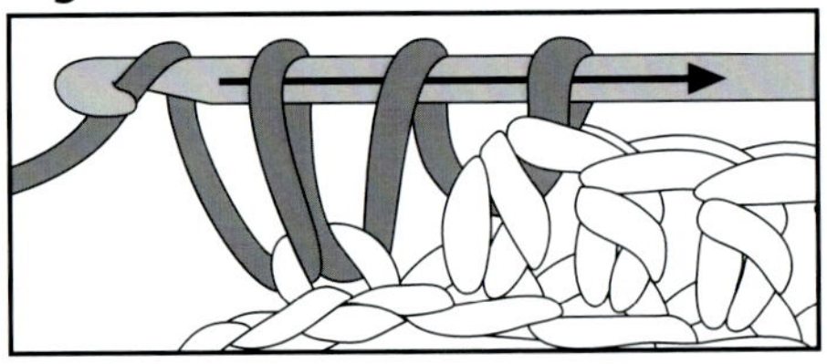

## DOUBLE CROCHET

YO, insert hook in stitch or space indicated, YO and pull up a loop (3 loops on hook), YO and draw through 2 loops on hook ***(Fig. 10a)***, YO and draw through remaining 2 loops on hook ***(Fig. 10b)*** **(double crochet made, *abbreviated dc*)**.

**Fig. 10a**

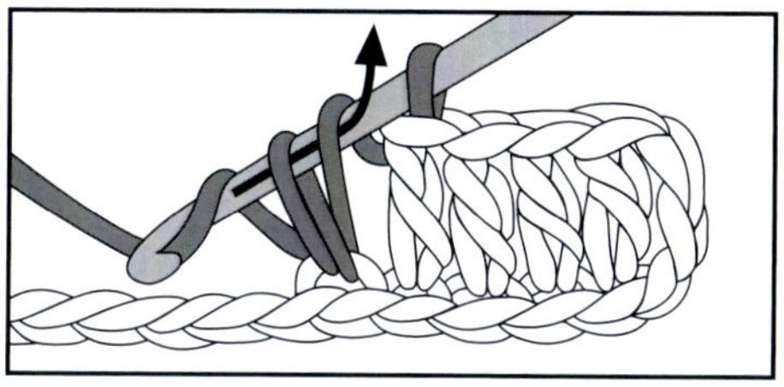

**Fig. 10b**

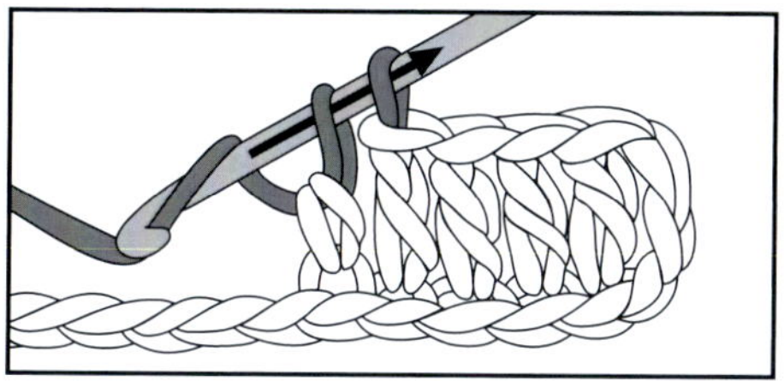

## TREBLE CROCHET

YO twice, insert hook in stitch or space indicated, YO and pull up a loop (4 loops on hook) ***(Fig. 11a)***, (YO and draw through 2 loops on hook) 3 times ***(Fig. 11b)*** **(treble crochet made, *abbreviated tr*)**.

**Fig. 11a**

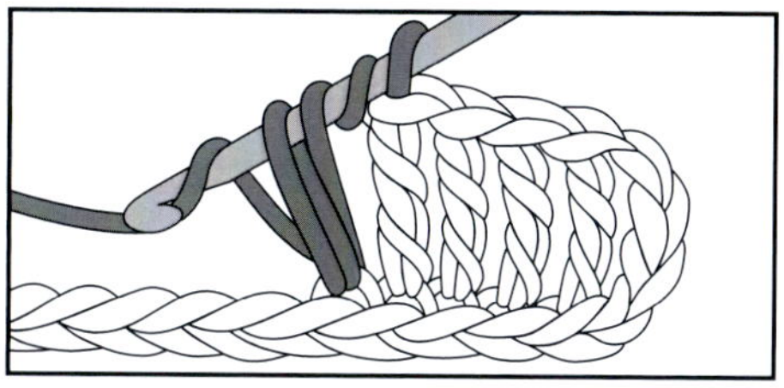

**Fig. 11b**

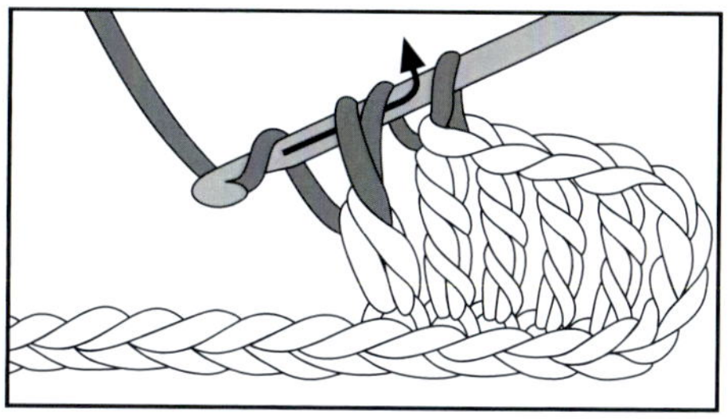

## DOUBLE TREBLE CROCHET

YO 3 times, insert hook in stitch or space indicated, YO and pull up a loop (5 loops on hook) ***(Fig. 12a)***, (YO and draw through 2 loops on hook) 4 times ***(Fig. 12b)*** **(double treble crochet made, *abbreviated dtr*)**.

**Fig. 12a**

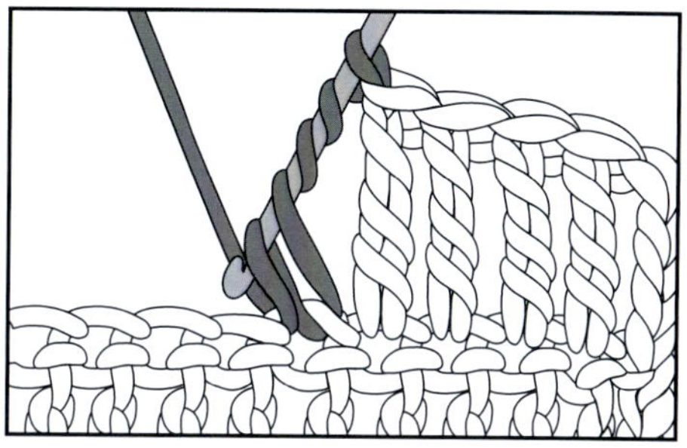

**Fig. 12b**

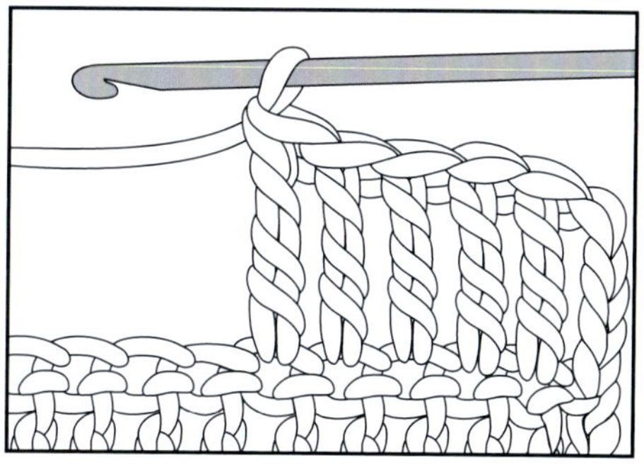

# Yarn Information

Each Afghan in this book was made using Medium Weight yarn. Any brand of Medium Weight yarn may be used. It is best to refer to the yardage/meters when determining how many balls or skeins to purchase. Remember, to arrive at the finished size, it is the GAUGE/TENSION that is important, not the brand of yarn.

For your convenience, listed in the following column are the specific yarn styles and colors used to create our photography models. Because yarn manufacturers make frequent changes in their product lines, you may sometimes find it necessary to use a substitute yarn or to search for the discontinued product at alternate suppliers (locally or online).

**SUGAR FREE**
***Premier® Ever Soft®***
Blue - #1138-20 Aqua
Pink - #1138-10 Magenta
Green - #1138-17 Lime Green

**BEACH VOLLEY**
***Red Heart® Super Saver®***
Variegated - #3944 Macaw
Blue - #0512 Turqua
Green - #0672 Spring Green

**OOPS MY NAILS**
***Red Heart® Soft®***
Purple - #9528 Lilac
Dk Pink - #9273 Very Pink

**SUPER DIVA**
***Cascade Yarns® 220 Superwash®***
Purple - #804 Amethyst
Dk Pink - #837 Berry Pink
Pink - #834 Strawberry Pink
Black - #815 Black

**PSYCHEDELIC**
***Red Heart® Super Saver®***
Blue - #0886 Blue
Yellow - #0324 Bright Yellow
Green - #0672 Spring Green
Pink - #0718 Shocking Pink

**SO FRESH**
***Premier® Anti-Pilling Everday® Worsted***
Orange - #100-54 Coral
Green - #100-38 Electric Green
Yellow - #100-27 Lemon

**MEETING THE PARALLELS**
***Premier® Ever Soft®***
Black - #1138-34 Black
Blue - #1138-23 Cornflower Blue
Pink - #1138-10 Magenta
Green - #1138-17 Lime Green
Yellow - #1138-12 Yellow

We have made every effort to ensure that theseinstructions are accurate and complete. We cannot, however, be responsible for human errortypographical mistakes, or variations in individual work.

Production Team:
Project Manager/Technical Editor - Linda A. Daley
Graphic Artist - Angela Ormsby Stark
Photo Stylist - Lori Wenger
Photographer - Jason Masters



Made in U.S.A.